The Wild West

Which of these two rootin'-tootin' cowpokes roped the moon? Who roped the sun?

Which hat appears the most along this border?

A TRIP TO THE ZOO

YIKES! THE ANIMALS HAVE TAKEN **LETTERS** FROM **SIGNS** AROUND THE **ZOO**! PLEASE MATCH THE **LETTER** TO EACH **ANIMAL** IN THE **BLANKS** TO ANSWER THIS QUESTION: **WHAT DO DOLPHINS WEAR TO KEEP WARM?**

CHANGE ONE LETTER PER WORD TO TRANSFORM THIS SWEET LITTLE DEER INTO A FEROCIOUS LION!!

DEER

_ _ _ _   TERM OF AFFECTION

_ _ _ _   SHAKESPEARE KING

_ _ _ _   TO REST ON

_ _ _ _   TO LEND MONEY

_ _ _ _   LARGE WATERBIRD

LION

CAN YOU FIND THE **ONE CAMEL** THAT MATCHES THIS **SHADOW** EXACTLY?

3

Answers on page 59.

Dive In!

Finish this scene with your favorite sea creatures
and other underwater treasures.

TREASURE HUNT

START YOUR QUEST FOR ANCIENT RICHES BY JUMPING FROM SKULL TO SKULL! EACH SKULL MUST HAVE EVEN-NUMBERED TEETH AND BE TOUCHING EACH OTHER. BE BRAVE!!

START

WHEW! YOU MADE IT TO THE TREASURE TROVE. THERE ARE 7 MATCHING PAIRS OF TREASURE CHESTS. FIND THEM, CROSS THEM OUT, AND THE ONE CHEST REMAINING IS THE ONE FILLED WITH TREASURE. YAHOO!

8

Answers on page 60.

ROYAL RESIDENCE

Journey to your new palace and create a castle fit for a King...or queen!

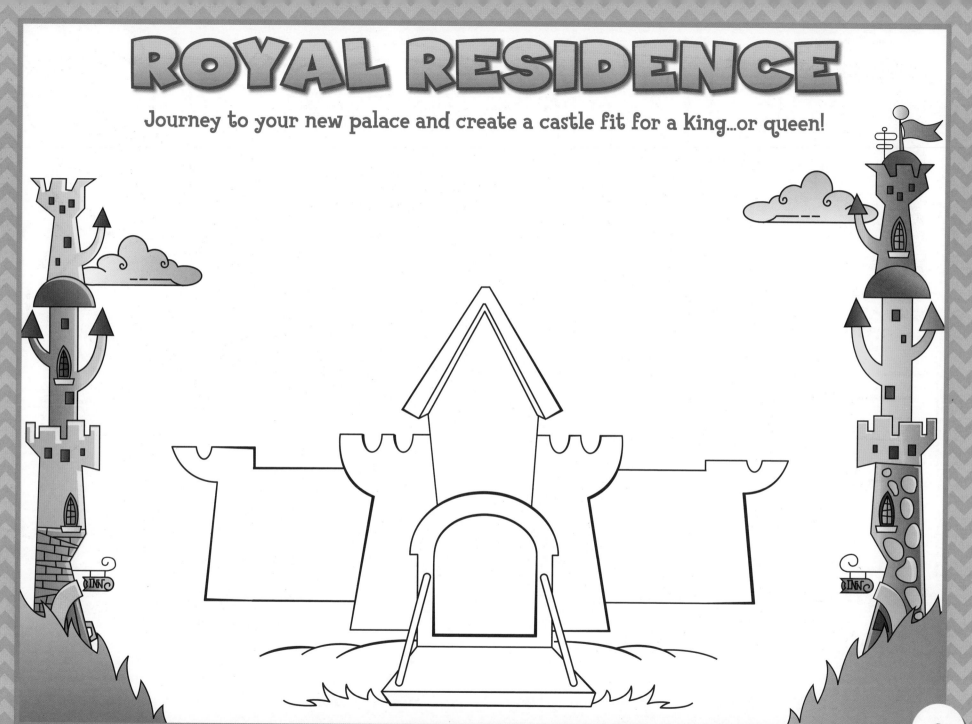

FINISH

Who's that cute bird sitting on the tree branch? Connect the dots and find out! Then, color as you like.

1 2 3 4 5 6 7 8 9 10 11 12 13 14 15 16 17 18 19 20 21 22 23 24 25 26

MONKEY

Only one shadow fits the monkey. Find it!

a b c

d e f

river danger

The explorer and his guide are traveling along the Amazon, but they don't know the way. Help them find the correct path!

START

find the differences

Look at the two river explorer illustrations. They are very similar, but they are different in 11 ways. Can you find them all?

AMAZON

RAIN FOREST

11

Answers on page 60.

ANTARCTICA ADVENTURE

There are 10  whales hidden in this picture. Can you find them?

Unscramble the letters below to find out what it's like in Antarctica.

FEZINEGR DOLC

_ _ _ _ _ _ _ _ _ _ _ _

Help Ziggy cross the floating ice so he can get to his mom.

START

END

12

Answers on page 60.

who's got the fish?
Seems like not everybody has been so lucky to catch a fish. Find out who is the lucky one!

Nice catch!
Dad is lucky! Connect the dots from 1 to 33 and then color in his catch.

the outsider
Find the one that doesn't fit among the others and circle it!

count 'em all!
Mom is checking if all her fish are accounted for. Help her to count them all and then circle the correct amount.

53 56 58

13

Answers on page 60.

TRIP TO EGYPT

LINK THE DOTS
What's the mysterious animal drinking by the oasis? Link the dots to find out.

NOT ONLY DESERT
The longest river in the world, the Nile, can be found in Egypt.

Find the two characters that look perfectly alike and circle them to open the temple's doors.

ESCAPE
Help the archaeologist escape from the scary mummy across the pyramid. There's only one way out. Find it!

start

finish

SPHINX
Ancient Egyptians used to build these huge statues, combining a lion's body with a Pharaoh's head. Have fun coloring it!

Across the USA

Which city is called "The Big Apple"?

Which state is the "Sunshine State"?

Which two states do not touch any other states?

Unscramble the letters below to spell out the names of seven states.

N O R A Z I A
G E R N O O
S A T E X
A G I M C H I N
A R I L F O D
T U A H
O L D A C O R O

Hint: Which city is called "The Windy City"?

Answers on page 61.

AFRICAN SAVANNA

Can you spot the seven differences between the mirror images of these animals?

ACROSS

3. King of the jungle
6. A big cat's shout
8. A spotted cat
9. Long, pointed ivory teeth
11. The predator stalks its _____
13. Long-necked animal

DOWN

1. It has horns on its nose
2. It has a trunk
4. Bristly African wild pig
5. Leopards have _____
7. Black and white horse
10. Black and white horse has these
12. Big reptile with long jaws
13. Antelope with long curved horns

Yikes! Look at all these animal tracks! Which **track** appears the **most**?

17

Answers on page 61.

THE RIGHT TRACK

Looks like the engineer needs some help! Find the way to the tunnel.

START

STATION

FINISH

WORD SEARCH

Find all the words listed below.

DRIVER
ENGINE
RAILROAD
STATION
TRAIN
WAGON

```
A S R B A O Y E V E
Y T R A I N M R A O
U Y O U I Z O G N Y
G B G C Y L B R O Z
I D R I V E R T I D
E V U M N S D O T C
R N V G U N O G A W
O A I B E I W C T D
T N T R A O I M S E
E U G N B S A W N U
```

CHOO CHOO CHOOSE

Only one of the shadows below matches the little train perfectly. Which one is it?

TRAIN TRIP

FIND THE DIFFERENCES

The two scenes are similar, but the second one has 10 differences. Circle them all!

RODEO FUN

START

BOOT MAZE
Find your way from start to finish!

FINISH

WORD SCRAMBLE
Unscramble the letters below to spell out the correct words!

TSOBO _ _ _ _ _

HESRO _ _ _ _ _

OSLAS _ _ _ _ _

BYOWCO _ _ _ _ _ _

THA _ _ _

DELDAS _ _ _ _ _ _

DIFFERENCES
The two cowboys below are very similar, but there are 11 differences between them. Find and circle them all.

CONFUSING HATS
So many hats! Only two of them are exactly the same. Can you spot them?

19

Answers on page 61.

TRIP TO NEW YORK

NY Times Crossword

Complete the names in the crossword spaces.

1. _____ State Building
2. _____ Square
3. Statue of _____
4. The Big _____
5. _____ way
6. Taxi _____

City Sudoku

Complete the grid below with the four landmarks. Each item should appear only once in every row, column, and square.

Central Park

Empire State Building

Guggenheim

Statue of Liberty

Lost in NYC
Find these objects:
cheese wedge
coffee mug
domino
horseshoe
paintbrush
paper clip
pencil
ship
stoplight

Gridlock
Get each cab to its waiting fare!

20

Answers on page 61.

Mad for Mexico

Aside from the many beaches, deserts, and mountains, Mexico is also known for its jungles. Unscramble the letters to spell out some animals that can be found in Mexico.

RODIECLOC
_____

RUJAAG
_____

RATPOR
_____

KOMYEN
_____

Can you name the four states that border Mexico?

MEXICAN SUDOKU

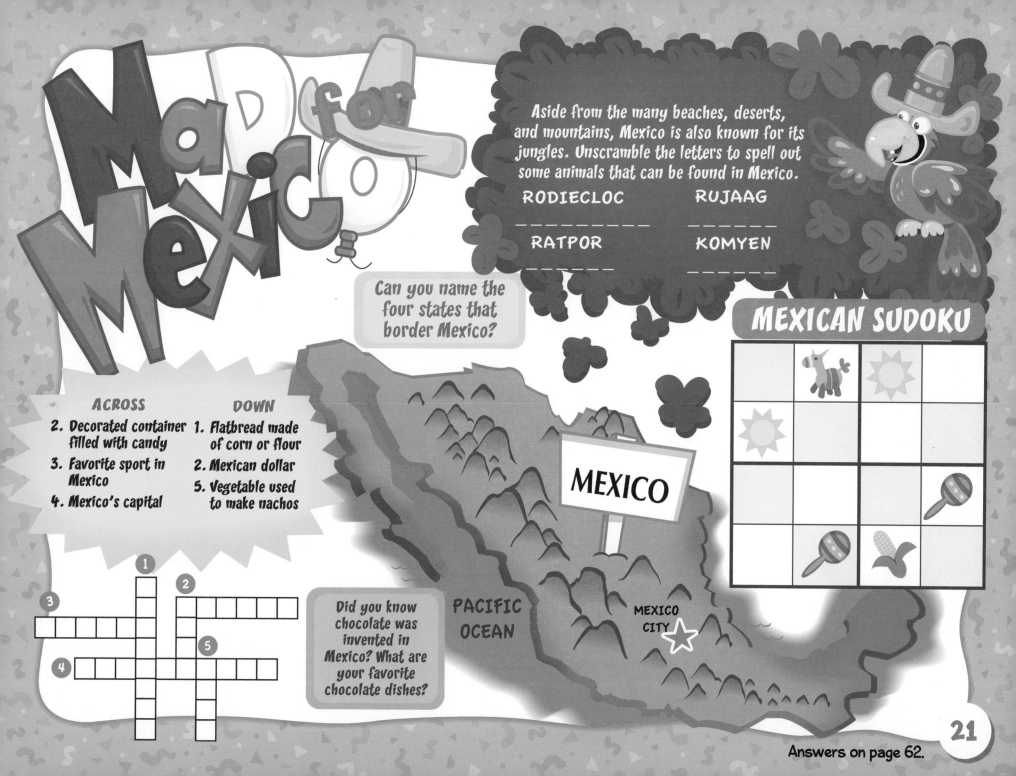

ACROSS
2. Decorated container filled with candy
3. Favorite sport in Mexico
4. Mexico's capital

DOWN
1. Flatbread made of corn or flour
2. Mexican dollar
5. Vegetable used to make nachos

MEXICO

Did you know chocolate was invented in Mexico? What are your favorite chocolate dishes?

PACIFIC OCEAN

MEXICO CITY

21

Answers on page 62.

RAIN FOREST FRIENDS

Complete the baby jaguar and baby gorilla in this scene.
Then draw other plants or animals you might
find in the rain forest.

22

Tookie Bird Safari

Help the explorers find the sneaky Tookie Bird.

START

FINISH

Answers on page 62.

OH MUMMY!

This mummy went on a trip, but he can't remember how to get home! Help him find his way, but first stop at the grocery store and then at the vet to pick up his pooch.

Finish

VET

Grocery

Start

FIND THE TWO CAMELS THAT MATCH!

1. 2. 3. 4. 5. 6. 7. 8. 9. 10.

24

Answers on page 62.

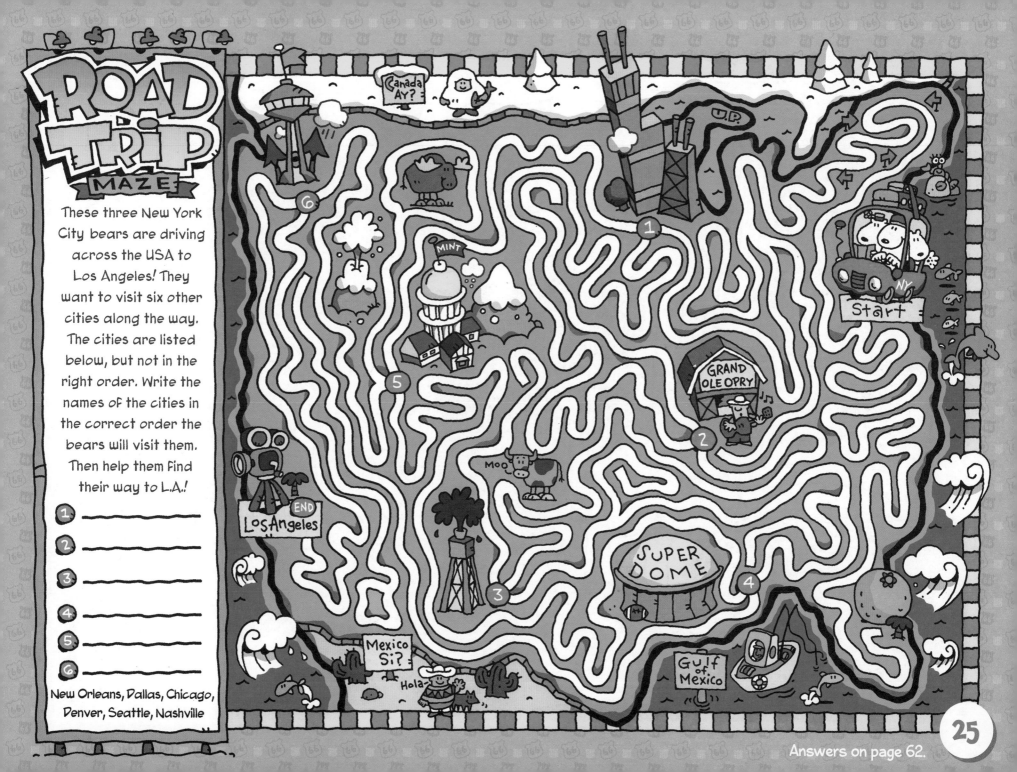

ROAD TRIP MAZE

These three New York City bears are driving across the USA to Los Angeles! They want to visit six other cities along the way. The cities are listed below, but not in the right order. Write the names of the cities in the correct order the bears will visit them. Then help them find their way to L.A.!

1 _____
2 _____
3 _____
4 _____
5 _____
6 _____

New Orleans, Dallas, Chicago, Denver, Seattle, Nashville

25

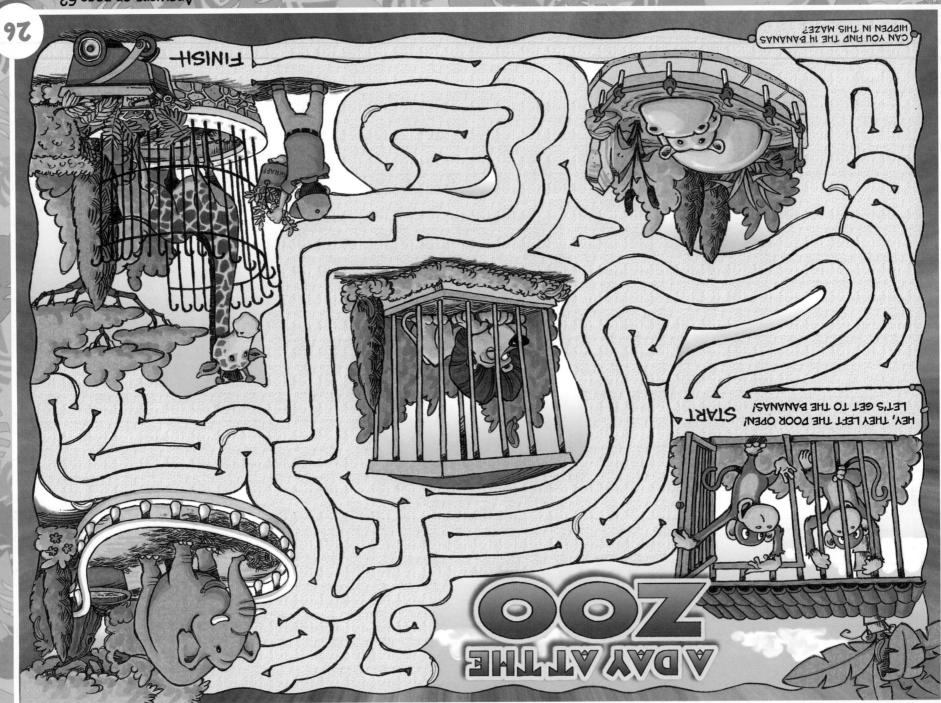

UP AND AWAY

Draw unique, colorful patterns in each hot air balloon. The sky's the limit with these doodles!

28

DOWNHILL RUN

Connect the dots, then color in the remainder of the scene!

29

Answers on page 63.

How many gold doubloons like this one can you find on this page?

Question: What did the ocean say to the sea captain?

Answer: Nothing. It just waved!

Arrrgghh!

"X" marks the spot! Sail ye ship to the treasure and make sure to stop for supplies once on each island... but be wary of sharks, skeletons, and sea monsters!!!

START

SUPPLIES

SUPPLIES

SUPPLIES

CITY LIFE

Turn this empty space into a bustling city filled with buildings, storefronts, people, and more.

LICENSE PLATE GAME

When you see a car's license plate, find your license plate sticker that matches the state and place it here!
Can you find all 50 states? For added fun we've added our neighbors Canada and Mexico!

ALABAMA	FLORIDA	KENTUCKY	MISSOURI	NORTH CAROLINA
ALASKA	GEORGIA	LOUISIANA	MONTANA	NORTH DAKOTA

ARIZONA	HAWAII	MAINE	NEBRASKA	OHIO	SOUTH DAKOTA	WASHINGTON
ARKANSAS	IDAHO	MARYLAND	NEVADA	OKLAHOMA	TENNESSEE	WEST VIRGINIA
CALIFORNIA	ILLINOIS	MASSACHUSETTS	NEW HAMPSHIRE	OREGON	TEXAS	WISCONSIN
COLORADO	INDIANA	MICHIGAN	NEW JERSEY	PENNSYLVANIA	UTAH	WYOMING
CONNECTICUT	IOWA	MINNESOTA	NEW MEXICO	RHODE ISLAND	VERMONT	CANADA
DELAWARE	KANSAS	MISSISSIPPI	NEW YORK	SOUTH CAROLINA	VIRGINIA	MEXICO

ARIZONA

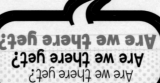
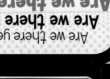

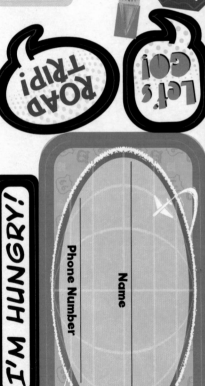
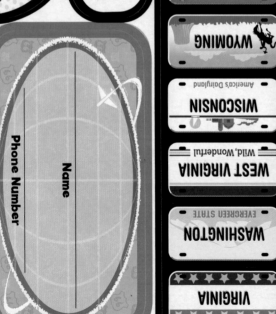

Use these stickers for the LICENSE PLATE GAME on page 32.

Luggage tag sticker

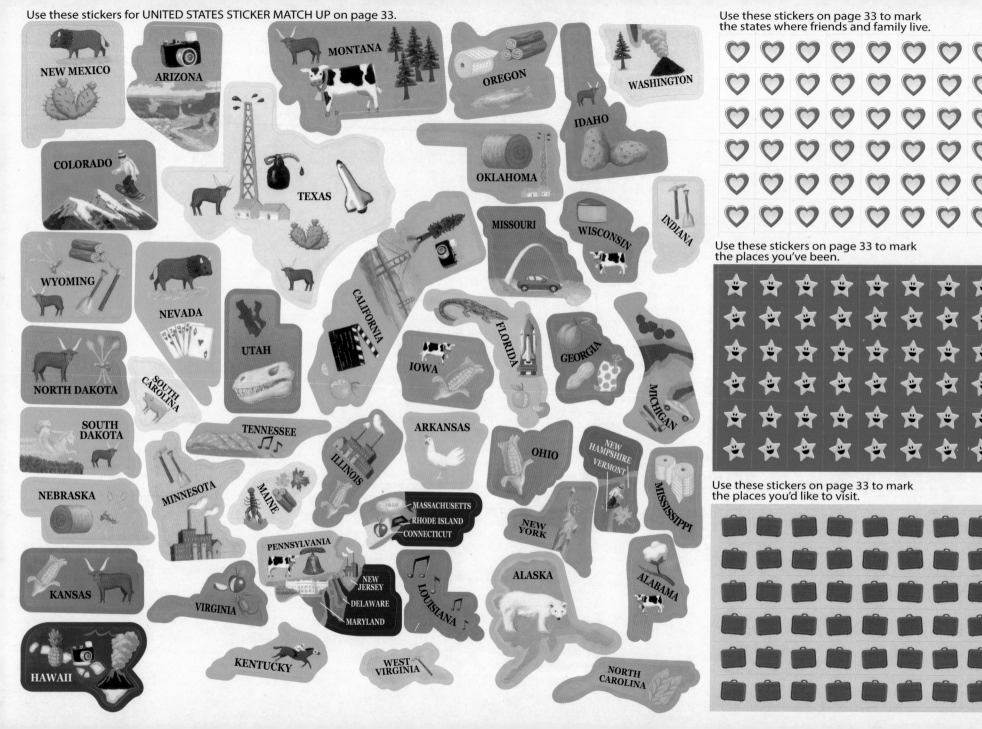

Use these stickers for UNITED STATES STICKER MATCH UP on page 33.

Use these stickers on page 33 to mark the states where friends and family live.

Use these stickers on page 33 to mark the places you've been.

Use these stickers on page 33 to mark the places you'd like to visit.

UNITED STATES STICKER MATCH UP

Help build America!
Find each state sticker and use them to fill in this map of the United States!

CANADA

Pacific
Ocean

Atlantic
Ocean

Gulf of Mexico

MEXICO

N
W E
S

Answers on page 63.

DEEP DIVE

Help the angelfish find his friends.

START

FINISH

Answers on page 63.

Connect the dots, then color in the remainder of the scene!

35

Connect the dots, then color in the remainder of the scene!

MUMMY MIA!

Connect the dots, then color in the remainder of the scene!

37

Happy Landings!

Connect the dots, then color in the remainder of the scene!

38

Ride 'em Cowboy!

Connect the dots, then color in the remainder of the scene!

40

Connect the dots, then color in the remainder of the scene!

41

RIDIN' THE RAILS

Connect the dots, then color in the remainder of the scene!

Connect the dots, then color in the remainder of the scene!

43

What Happens Next?

Tell the story of this vacationing family by doodling the rest of this comic strip.

VISITORS FROM **outer space**

Connect the dots
to draw the alien spaceship.

Use the code to solve
this message.

**What kind of pet
would an alien get?
Draw an alien pet below.**

A B C D E F G H I J K L M N O P Q R S T U V W X Y Z

45

Answers on page 63.

SEA SURPRISE

Connect the dots, then color in the remainder of the scene!

46

EVEREST CHALLENGE

Help these climbers to the top of the world! Be sure to stop at each campsite along the way.

Mt. Everest

Watch Your Step!

GO BACK

B

C

A

Start

Climbing BONUS

Only six rocks on this climb have numbers that don't touch a rock with the same number. Can you find them?

47

Answers on page 63.

Answers on page 63.

Start

Find

FLYING BEARS

FLEA

NO WAY!

10

10

The HUMAN CANNON BALL!

☆ Challenge! ☆

The Flying Bears are ready to perform, but one of their members is still on the ground! Help this bear choose the right rope for his climb up top!

Big Top

FLYING BEARS

FLY BEA

Finish

Answers on page 64.

On
BROADWAY

The spotlight is on! Draw yourself dancing, acting, singing—whatever your talent—on this stage.

Connect the dots, then color in the remainder of the scene!

51

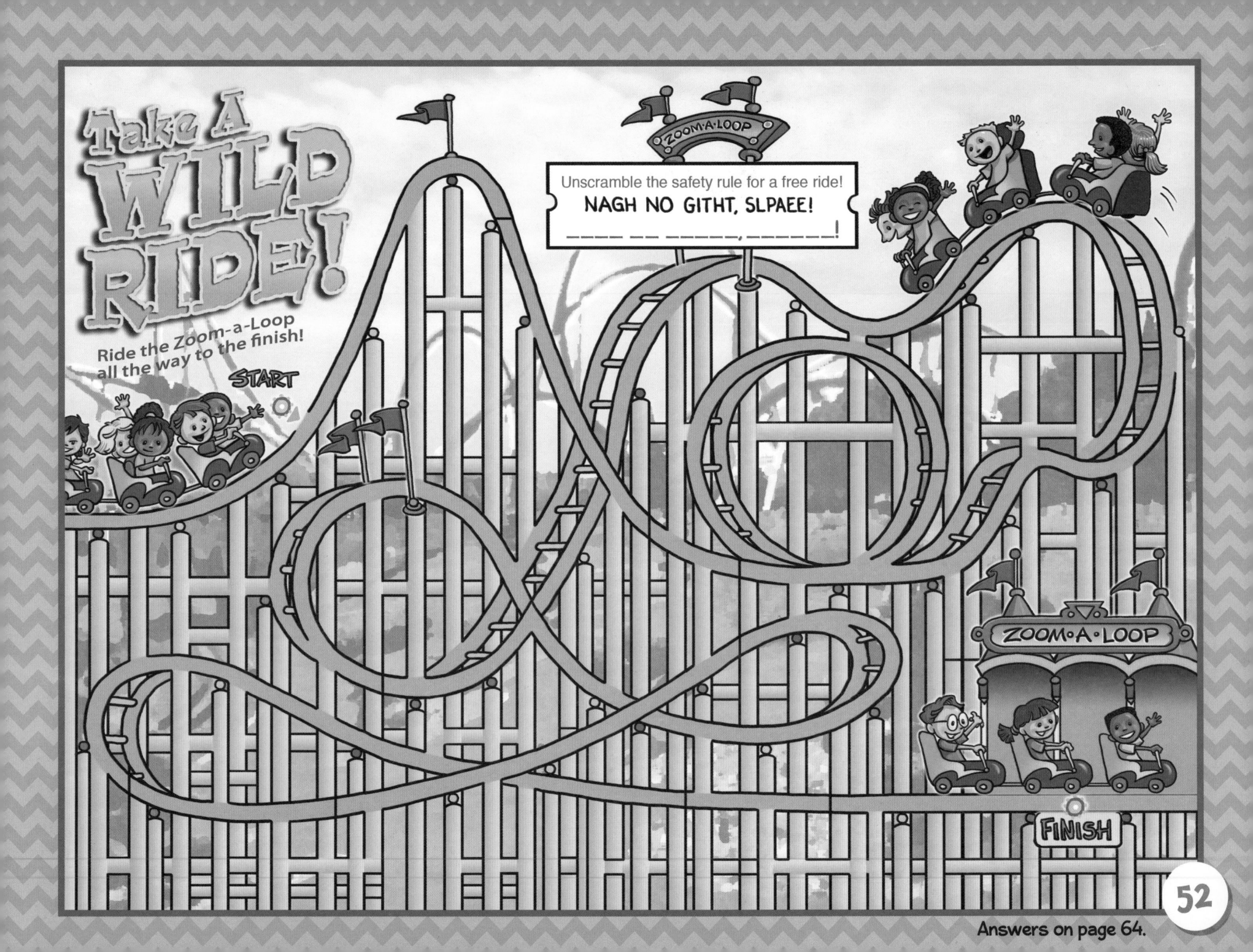

Take A WILD RIDE!

Ride the Zoom-a-Loop all the way to the finish!

START

Unscramble the safety rule for a free ride!

NAGH NO GITHT, SLPAEE!

_____ __ _____, _____!

ZOOM·A·LOOP

FINISH

52

Answers on page 64.

Answers on page 64.

All Aboard!

Draw this train engine in five steps as it pulls into the station. Add train cars for even more doodle fun.

ALIEN INTELLIGENCE

Connect the dots, then color in the remainder of the scene!

All Hands on Deck

Connect the dots, then color in the remainder of the scene!

Going Bananas

Finish the rest of this gorilla, using the first half as a guide.

Time Travel

Connect the dots, then color in the remainder of the scene!

58

Page 1
A Day in the City

Page 2
The Wild West

Page 3
A Trip to the Zoo

Page 4
A Day at the Museum

Page 5
A Day at the Beach

Page 7
Under the Sea

Answers

Page 8
Treasure Hunt

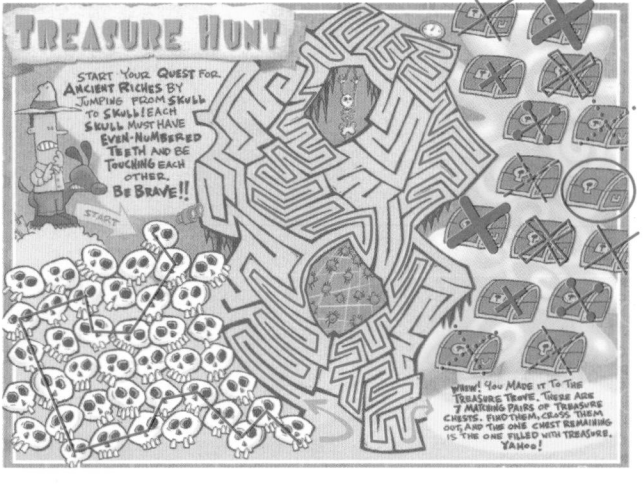

Page 10
Jungle Exploration

Page 11
Rain Forest

Page 12
Antarctica Adventure

Page 13
Gone Fishin'

Page 14
Space Exploration

Page 15
Trip to Egypt

Page 16
Across the USA

OLDACORO .... COLORADO
TUAH .... UTAH
ARILFOD .... FLORIDA
AGIMCHIN .... MICHIGAN
SATEX .... TEXAS
GERNOO .... OREGON
NORAZIA .... ARIZONA

Which two states do not touch any other states?
ALASKA HAWAII

Which state is the "Sunshine State"? FLORIDA

Which city is called "The Big Apple"? NEW YORK

Page 17
African Savanna

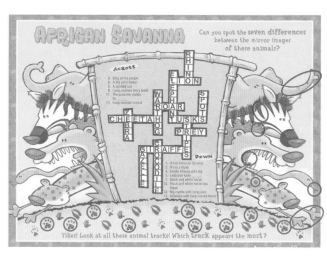

Page 18
Train Trip

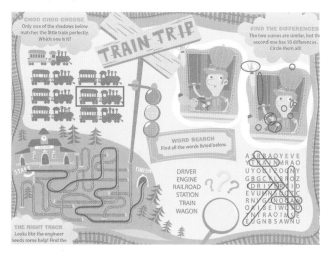

DRIVER
ENGINE
RAILROAD
STATION
TRAIN
WAGON

Page 19
Rodeo Fun

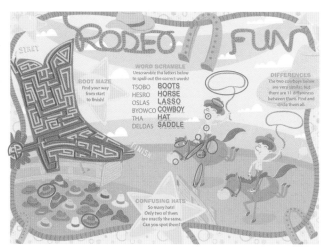

TSOBO — BOOTS
HESRO — HORSE
OSLAS — LASSO
BYOWCO — COWBOY
THA — HAT
DELDAS — SADDLE

Page 20
Trip to New York

Page 21
Mad Mexico

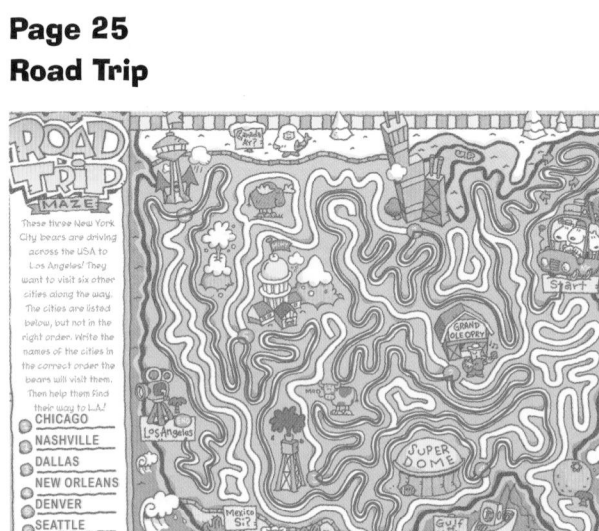

Page 23
Tookie Bird

Page 24
Oh Mummy

Page 25
Road Trip

Page 26
A Day at the Zoo

Page 27
River Runners